WEIRD ANIMAL SCIENCE

PACK ANIMALS

THE BREAKDOWN

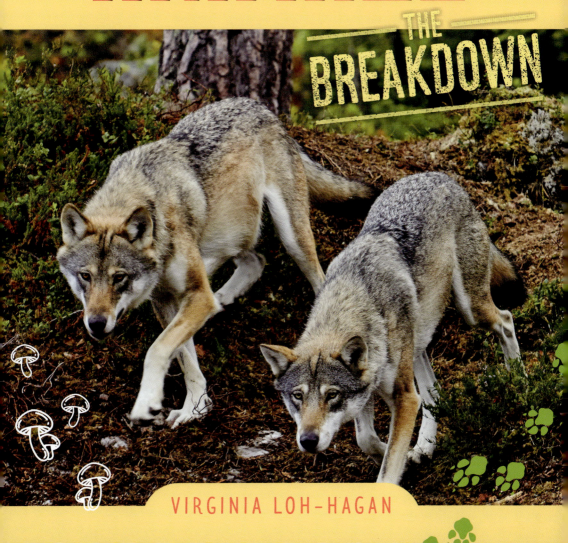

VIRGINIA LOH-HAGAN

45TH PARALLEL PRESS

Published in the United States of America by Cherry Lake Publishing Group
Ann Arbor, Michigan
www.cherrylakepublishing.com

Photo Credits: © Michal Martinek/Shutterstock, cover, 1; © bsd studio/Shutterstock, cover, 1, 8; © Lars Poyansky/Shutterstock, cover, 1; © melissamn/Shutterstock, 6; © In Art/Shutterstock, 7; © Benmo/Shutterstock, 9; © matthieu Gallet/Shutterstock, 10; © wildestanimal/Shutterstock, 12; © Geoffrey Kuchera/Shutterstock, 14; © Martin Prochazkacz/Shutterstock, 16; © Iconic Bestiary/Shutterstock, 17; © Holly Kuchera/Shutterstock, 19; © Tomas Hejlek/Shutterstock, 21

Graphic Element Credits: Graphic Element Credits: Cover, multiple interior pages: © WindAwake/Shutterstock; © Theo_hrm/Shutterstock; © Rodin Anton/Shutterstock; © Petr Vaclavek/Shutterstock; © Nikolaeva/Shutterstock

45th Parallel Press is an imprint of Cherry Lake Publishing Group.

Library of Congress Cataloging-in-Publication Data has been filed and is available at catalog.loc.gov

Cherry Lake Publishing Group would like to acknowledge the work of the Partnership for 21st Century Learning, a Network of Battelle for Kids. Please visite Battelle for Kids online for more information.

Printed in the United States of America

Note from publisher: Websites change regularly, and their future contents are outside of our control. Supervise children when conducting any recommended online searches for extended learning opportunities.

Dr. Virginia Loh-Hagan is an author, university professor, and former classroom teacher. She's currently the Director of the Asian Pacific Islander Desi American Resource Center at San Diego State University. She loves science-fiction stories. She lives in San Diego with her very tall husband and very naughty dogs.

TABLE OF CONTENTS

BREAK IT DOWN

1. DECODE IT
- Look at each letter.
- Look at letter patterns.
- Blend sounds.
- Try other possible sounds.

2. BUILD VOCABULARY
- Listen to the word.
- Match the sounds to a word you know.
- Look for context clues for words you don't know.
- Look up the meaning in a glossary or dictionary.

3. MAKE CONNECTIONS
- Name other examples.
- Draw the idea.
- Compare ideas.
- Ask questions.

TEST IT OUT

WORDS YOU'LL LEARN

Look over the list of vocabulary words. Are there any you already know?

breed   evolved
dominant   pack
enough

GET STARTED

Open and closed syllables are 2 types of syllables. Open syllables end with a long vowel. Closed syllables end with a consonant. They have a short vowel sound.

- Look at the letters.
- Divide words into syllables.
- Try dividing another way if needed.

The word *dominant* starts with a closed syllable. It is pronounced: DAHM-uh-nuhnt.

- The 1st vowel is a short *o*: *dahm-*.
- The 2nd and 3rd vowels say "uh": *-uh-nuhnt*.

Your family or friends are your **pack**.

Some animals have packs.

Packs are groups of wild animals.

They live together. They hunt together.

Animals live in packs for different reasons.

They defend themselves.

They join forces to attack prey.

They work together to gather food.

They help care for the young.

Sometimes, the pack causes problems.

Packs can get too big. There may not be **enough** food. Enough means the right amount.

DECODE IT

The word *enough* has 2 vowel sounds. The 1st syllable is an open syllable. The *gh* says "fff."

- Break it into chunks: e-nough.

- The 1st vowel sound is a long *e*.

- The next vowel sound says "uh."

- *Enough* is pronounced ee-NUHF.

Many animals live in packs.

An elephant's pack is called a herd.

A lion's pack is called a pride.

A whale's pack is called a pod.

Many animals **evolved** to live in packs. This means changed over time.

This was the best way for them to survive.

Wolves are known for being pack animals.

They work together to take down bigger prey.

DECODE IT

The word *evolved* has 2 vowel sounds. The 1st syllable is an open syllable.

- The 1st vowel sound is a long *e*.

- The next vowel sound says "aw."

- *Evolved* is pronounced ee-VAWLVD.

Wolf packs are related by blood.

There's an order of who is in charge.

Most wolf packs have 10 to 15 members.

Each pack has a **dominant** pair. That means in charge.

They lead the hunts.

They eat first when a kill is made.

BUILD VOCABULARY

Breed (BREED) means to make babies.

- All animals breed to have babies.

- Most animals need female and male partners to breed. Some fish and lizards can breed without a partner.

- Other forms: breeding, breeder, dying breed

They **breed**. Breed means to make babies. They are usually the parents of the pack.

The babies grow up. They stay 1 to 2 years.

They help care for younger siblings.

MAKE CONNECTIONS

Many animals form packs. Humans form packs.

- Why might humans form packs?

- What can human packs look like? What are they called?

Young adult wolves often leave.

They find mates. They start new packs.

PUT IT TOGETHER

Detail:
Packs work together to hunt or gather food.

Detail:
Wolf packs are related by blood.

Detail:
Packs help take care of babies.

Main Idea:
Animals live in packs for many reasons.

Detail:
Elephants, lions, whales, and wolves have packs.

Detail:
Packs may separate if they get too big.

LEARN MORE

BOOKS

Jenkins, Steve. *The Animals Book*. Boston, MA: HMH Books for Young Readers, 2013.

Lerwill, Ben, and Sarah Walsh (illus.). *WildLives: 50 Extraordinary Animals That Made History*. New York, NY: Atheneum Books for Young Readers, 2020.

Watson, Galadriel, and Samantha Dixon (illus.) *Running Wild: Awesome Animals in Motion*. Toronto, ON: Annick Press, 2020.

ONLINE

Search these online sources with an adult:
- National Geographic Kids | Animals
- Britannica Kids | Animal Kingdom

GLOSSARY

breed (BREED) to mate in order to make babies

dominant (DAH-muh-nuhnt) in charge

enough (ee-NUHF) the right amount

evolved (ee-VAWLVD) changed over time

pack (PAK) a tight family unit

INDEX